ETIQUETTE RULES!™

CROSS-CULTURAL ETIQUETTE

AVERY ELIZABETH HURT

rosen publishing's
rosen central®

NEW YORK

Published in 2017 by The Rosen Publishing Group, Inc.
29 East 21st Street, New York, NY 10010

Library of Congress Cataloging-in-Publication Data

Names: Hurt, Avery, author.
Title: Cross-cultural etiquette / Avery Elizabeth Hurt.
Description: First Edition. | New York : Rosen Publishing, 2017. | Series: Etiquette rules! | Includes bibliographical references and index.
Identifiers: LCCN 2016017415 | ISBN 9781499464986 (library bound) | ISBN 9781499464962 (pbk.) | ISBN 9781499464979 (6-pack)
Subjects: LCSH: Etiquette for children and teenagers--Juvenile literature.
Classification: LCC BJ1857.C5 H87 2016 | DDC 395.1/22—dc23
LC record available at https://lccn.loc.gov/2016017415

Manufactured in China

CONTENTS

INTRODUCTION

" Etiquette" is a fancy word for good manners. It may make you think of complicated rules about silverware or chewing with your mouth closed, and while those sorts of things are certainly a part of etiquette, they aren't what etiquette is fundamentally about. Etiquette is really about kindness— making other people comfortable, whether you're in their space or they're in yours.

Making sure everyone is comfortable sometimes does require paying attention to things like, yes, which fork to use or when to take off your hat. That's because those small things that people do (and don't do) send out a lot of subtle messages. If you don't know the culture of the people around you, you might be sending a totally different message than you think you're sending. In some cultures, cleaning your plate shows that you're grateful for the food. In other cultures, it just makes you look greedy. This may seem like a small thing, but big things are made up of small things, and getting along with other people and showing them that you respect them is a big thing.

So why is all this so complicated? That's because etiquette is different from culture to culture. Culture is simply the character-istics of a group of people; things like how they talk and dress, what they eat and who they worship, and what kinds of art and music they make. A group can be anything from a huge nation, like China or India, to the people in the debate club at your school.

For much of history, most people lived their entire lives in one culture. But these days, people move around and cultures overlap. North America is particularly rich in cultural diversity: Latinos, African Americans, Asian Americas, European Americans,

The world is filled with many different kinds of people. Learning how to get along so that everyone feels comfortable is what etiquette is really about.

Creoles, Cajuns, Canadians, French Canadians, Jews, Mormons, Muslims, Christians, jocks, nerds, tech geeks, and artists—you get the idea. During your life, you are likely to meet people from all over the world, not just North America. According to a 2014 report published by ITB-Berlin, the world's largest international trade fair, young people are traveling more and farther than ever before. We all need to pay attention to everyone else's customs so we will know how to make each other feel comfortable wherever we are.

This book is not an exhaustive guide to the etiquette practices of the many cultures of the world. But it will help you understand a little more about other people's customs, how to behave in lots of different situations, as well as how to make things better when you blow it (because when it comes to cross-cultural etiquette, everybody blows it now and then). And learning about it is a lot of fun (where else will you read about when it's perfectly okay to burp at the table?).

Respecting the many cultures around you will help foster cross-cultural brotherhood and sisterhood on a global scale. By getting these small things right, you are helping to create a better world.

CHAPTER ONE

GETTING ACQUAINTED

The first thing you usually say when you meet someone new is "Hello. Nice to meet you."

Or maybe, "Hey, dude, what's up?"

Then you shake hands or give a big high-five.

You already know that different situations call for different types of greetings. But did you know that across the world, and even across the United States, there are many ways to say hello? Knowing how to say hello is one of the first steps to good etiquette.

GETTING IN TOUCH—OR NOT!

Most people in North America are pretty relaxed about friendly touching. Handshakes are often the most polite way to greet someone even if you do not

Sports teams often have unique ways of greeting each other and celebrating. Sometimes these slaps and shakes make their way into the non-sports world.

7

know them well, and pats on the back are common. Many people, especially Hispanics who are comfortable with closer personal space, often hug each other when they meet. But some people feel uncomfortable with touching. Many Asians prefer to bow to one another. Japanese people give a brief nod when greeting friends and family and a deeper bow on more formal occasions. When you meet people from Asia, it's wise to give them a little space and not a good idea to insist on a handshake.

Most Europeans feel comfortable with handshakes. In many parts of Europe, people give each other a quick kiss on the cheek when they meet. It may seem odd, though, that in cultures where it is customary to kiss cheeks when meeting, hugging is often thought to be too much of an invasion of personal space.

HOW MUCH IS TOO MUCH?

If you're having trouble knowing what is and is not the right amount of touching, don't feel bad. Even heads of state sometimes have trouble with this one. In 2006, then president George W. Bush entered a meeting of world leaders and when he walked by the German chancellor, Angela Merkel, already seated at the table, he gave her a friendly shoulder squeeze. Germans are not comfortable with that kind of spontaneous touching—especially in such formal settings. The German leader responded with surprise, jumping in her chair and looking a bit miffed. Merkel laughed about it later, though, and she and President Bush remained on good terms.

WHO ARE YOU LOOKING AT?

Sometimes a gesture that is required in one culture can be offensive in another. In most of the United States and in parts of Europe, looking someone directly in the eye when you meet them is a good thing. But making too much eye contact is considered rude and possibly even aggressive. Even within the United States, different cultures have different—and some-times very subtle—opinions about eye contact. People in the South and the West Coast tend to glance at (and often say hello to) strangers when passing them on the street. This sometimes puzzles people from other parts of the country and can make them uncomfortable.

RESPECT YOUR ELDERS

Most people in the United States are comfortable with at least some informality between generations, but in many European cultures and in all Asian and Hispanic cultures, showing respect for older people is extremely important.

Fortunately, this is an area where it is hard to go wrong. It's always safe to treat adults with an added measure of respect, calling them by their last names and titles (Mr., Mrs., Ms., Professor, or Doctor), and letting them set the tone for your interactions. If adults prefer less formality, they'll certainly let you know.

If all this sounds like you are in for a culture clash before you've even gotten to know someone, don't panic. The best thing to do when you first meet people is to follow their lead. If they hug you, you, hug them back. If they bow, bow in return. Always keep a comfortable distance until you are

SAYING HELLO

The things people do when they run into a friend or meet someone new get way more creative than just shaking hands or bowing. The Maoris, the indigenous people of New Zealand, greet each other by rubbing noses. In Tibet, people stick out their tongues when they run into friends. The Inuits of Greenland press their noses against the other person's skin and breathe on them. In parts of Niger, people shake their fists beside their heads and say, "Wooshay, Wooshay," (which means "hello") when they meet. You may even have some unique and personal ways you greet your friends or family.

A Maori man greets a Brazilian native with the traditional Hongi greeting—touching noses and foreheads. This is the Maori equivalent of a handshake.

THERE'S A WORD FOR THAT

Differences in how you treat people based on their age or relationship to you are so much a part of some cultures that they are built into the language. In Spanish, for example, the English word "you" becomes *tú* if you are talking with a friend or relative. But in more formal situations, like when you're talking with a teacher, someone who is much older than you, or someone you do not know well, you would use the Spanish word *ustéd*. Many languages have these degrees of formality built in as a way of showing respect, and figuring out when to use the formal and when not to can cause some etiquette problems even within cultures.

sure how the person feels about being touched. Be especially respectful toward older people. And don't panic if you get something wrong. Just apologize sincerely, and ask people what makes them comfortable. Letting others know that you care about their feelings—and their culture—is one of the best ways to make friends.

CHAPTER TWO

IN CLASS

H iro arrives early for the first day of science class, hangs his jacket neatly on the back of his chair, and carefully arranges his paper and pencils on the desk in front of him. Sarah comes in a few minutes later, tosses her jacket over the back of her chair, drops her backpack on top of the desk, and props her sneaker-clad feet on the empty chair in front of her. Luis rushes in just as the bell is ringing, jokingly pushes Sarah's feet out of the chair, and is still joking around with Sarah when the math teacher, Ms. Austin, arrives. As soon as Ms. Austin comes into the room, Hiro leaps up from his desk and stands beside it, looking directly at Ms. Austin. The rest of the class laughs.

Hiro is an exchange student from Japan. At his school back home, everyone stands and greets the teacher when he or she enters. It is a way of showing respect. If the rest of the class had known this, they might not have laughed and embarrassed Hiro on his first day in a U.S. school. When students from many backgrounds are in school together, mutual respect and understanding can help everyone feel comfortable. Here are a few cultural differences that might show up in the classroom—and how to deal with them.

13

PICK ME!

Students in the United States are comfortable both answering and asking questions and are usually quite willing to challenge the teacher if something doesn't make sense or they disagree with something he or she says. But in many cultures speaking out in class or raising your hand to be called on to give an answer or ask a question is considered pushy, and challenging the teacher is completely unacceptable. In Thailand, for example, when a student asks many questions, the teacher can get

Even when and when not to raise your hand in class can have cultural variations. What seems like eager interest to one person might seem like showing off to another.

the idea that the student doesn't understand the material and label the student as a slow learner. Thai students are hesitant to ask questions and give the teacher the wrong impression. Chinese students often think that participating too much in class will make it look like they are showing off. It can seem as if these students don't care about school when something totally different is actually going on.

Even when students from other cultures are willing to speak up in class, taking turns can sometimes be tricky for them. It may seem clear to U.S. students when a speaker has come to the end of his or her point and it's okay to jump in with a question or comment. But for students unfamiliar with the give and take of U.S. conversation and for those whose first language is not English, taking part in a class discussion might be overwhelming. Also, many Asian cultures value teamwork over individual accomplishment. The U.S. emphasis on personal achievement can seem excessively competitive to many Asians. The spirited back-and-forth that characterizes many U.S. classroom discussions can be disturbing to Asian students, who tend to be uncomfortable with conflict and value harmony and cooperation over argument and competition. No wonder they stay quiet during classroom discussions!

LATE AGAIN

The way people think about time also varies from culture to culture, and this can cause problems in the classroom. People in the United States tend to see time as a limited resource, place a high value on their time, and think that it is rude to be even a few minutes late. In Hispanic, Arabic, Asian, and many African cultures, people tend to think of time as secondary to people and relationships. They are much more flexible about

An American student—in a culture where time is valued highly and being late is considered rude—rushes through the halls to make it to class on time.

deadlines and are less concerned about "wasting" time. People from these cultures think of delays and interruptions to schedules as just a part of life and believe that it is more important for everyone to be comfortable than to get everything done on schedule. The difference between being chronically late and being reasonably on time might come down to a cultural difference. Remember when Luis skidded into math class just as the bell rang? Luis is Mexican American; being late is not such a big deal in his culture.

School is, in many ways, a microcosm of the world, and,

TEAMWORK

Imagine that you are assigned to work on a science project with Luis, Hiro, Sarah, and Grace, who is from Sudan. Hiro understands the material well, but he is uncomfortable speaking up and taking charge. Luis is great at explaining concepts to everyone else, but he is late to all the meetings. Grace is creative but can't be counted on to finish her part of the project on time. Sarah is relaxed and informal (which makes Hiro uncomfortable) but gets testy and bossy when others are late to meetings or miss deadlines. Not only is your group in danger of failing because you can't complete your assignment, the atmosphere is tense and no one seems to be getting along. You can help with all this by making sure everyone else understands where the rest of the group is coming from. And then you can all make some accommodations.

as such, it is a great place for working out cultural differences in a safe environment. Simply being aware of why your fellow students behave the way they do goes a long way in smoothing out the differences. Getting to know your classmates and being interested in their lives and backgrounds is the best way to develop this awareness.

CHAPTER THREE

GUYS AND GALS

G ender issues are tricky enough even within cultures. When it comes to cross-cultural relationships, things can get unpredictable indeed. A little cultural sensitivity can make navigating the gender gap a little less difficult.

In much of the Western world, the gender gap has narrowed considerably, and men and women are considered equal, or at least mostly equal, in many cultures. But in many places, women are still expected to do different jobs and behave differently from men, and women often have fewer rights and opportunities.

UNDER THE VEIL

Though women in Muslim countries often do not have the same rights as men, women are not totally without power in the Muslim world. Women serve in the parliaments of Turkey, Egypt, Iraq, and Jordan. Muslim women, such as Benazir Bhutto of Pakistan, and Megawati Sukarnoputri, of Indonesia, have been leaders of their countries. It's important to understand that how much freedom and independence a Muslim woman has depends more on the country and social class she is from and the attitude of her family than solely on the fact that she is Muslim. Don't assume that just because a girl is Muslim that she will be timid and quiet. However, many Muslims do adhere to strict rules about interactions between the sexes.

Inequality between the sexes is subtler in Asian countries, but for the most part, women in Asia are less likely to be in positions of power and are generally subordinate to, or have less authority than, men both in the family and in the business world. Asian women will typically defer to men in conversations, and Asian girls might expect to be taken less seriously and valued less than boys.

Benazir Bhutto, two-time Prime Minister of Pakistan, is one of many Muslim women in leadership roles.

Hispanics often have a family structure in which the man is considered the head of the household and the woman is in charge of cooking, cleaning, and child care. Some religious groups, such as Mormons and fundamentalist Christians, consider women subordinate to men. But again, how closely individuals adhere to these teachings varies widely from group to group and even from family to family.

DATING

Inequality between men and women is especially tricky when it comes to cross-cultural dating. Many Muslims don't date at all, so don't take it personally if you're turned down by a Muslim classmate you would like to go out with. Try to be respectful of his or her feelings, too. It's not always easy to not take part in something everyone else is enjoying. If you don't know the cultural practices of someone you are interested in dating, it is a good idea to ask before making assumptions.

You might not have dating on your mind, but someone else might think you do. Attitudes and clothing that seem perfectly

In today's multicultural world, couples are often not only from different countries, but from totally different cultures as well. And they can make it work.

harmless in most cultures can be seen as flirtatious to men from some Middle Eastern cultures. A girl might smile and make a joke just to be friendly, but to these men it might seem as if she has made a romantic or sexual overture, or offer. When these misunderstandings happen, explain that you were just being friendly. Be polite, but clear. Sometimes men from these cultures think that women say no when they really mean yes. Make it clear that you mean exactly what you say.

Views about homosexuality vary from culture to culture. Things are improving for LGBTQ people in most cultures, but they often still struggle to be accepted.

Many cultures still disapprove of homosexual relationships. If you are lesbian, gay, bisexual, transgendered, or queer (or questionig, LGBTQ), you already know how difficult this can be. Trying to understand the pressure your classmates may be feeling from their cultures might help some. You don't have to change or hide who you are to make other people feel comfortable, but being understanding of others is often the best way to persuade them to understand you.

TEN QUESTIONS TO ASK AN ETIQUETTE EXPERT

1. What if I am allergic to the foods being offered at a meal? How do I politely refuse?
2. Should I try to learn a few phrases in other languages? Do I risk offending someone by not getting it right?
3. I want to ask someone out on a date, but I'm not sure of his or her cultural practices about dating. What should I do?
4. I'm open to different cultures, but my parents, not so much. I'm afraid to invite my friends from other cultures to my home because my parents might offend them. What should I do?
5. I think I have offended someone accidentally, but I'm not sure. Will I make things worse if I bring it up?
6. The girls in my neighborhood wear shorts when we're just hanging out. Some of the guys in the neighborhood are from Middle Eastern countries, and they call us whores and hookers because of the way we dress. I understand they have different expectations about dress, but the way they talk to us makes me uncomfortable. How should I respond?
7. I am invited to a Jewish wedding. I'm thinking of skipping because I don't know how to behave. What should I do?
8. Lots of the kids at my school are Mexican and speak Spanish to each other at lunch. It makes me uncomfortable to not understand what they're saying. I'm studying Spanish, but they speak way too fast for me. Would it be rude to ask them to speak English?
9. I am not a Christian and am uncomfortable when asked to join in prayer, such as at ballgames, or when people offer to pray for me. Is it okay to say, "No, thanks"?
10. My parents do not speak English well. This embarrasses me. How can I be more comfortable when my friends are around my parents?

CHAPTER FOUR

DRESS CODE

You probably already know that your clothes make a statement about you—even when there is nothing printed on your t-shirt—but you may not have realized that the statement is not just about who you are; it also about how you feel about other people. Just as etiquette is more a matter of kindness than of rules, what to wear and how you dress at certain occasions is more about respect than about dress codes. Dressing appropriately for an occasion shows that you respect the people you are with and the situation you are in. When the people you are with are from a different culture, the messages can become even more garbled. Your clothing may say something that you'd never in a million years thought of saying with your

Business people usually have dress codes for work, but these can vary from office to office and situation to situation.

SYSTEMS OF STYLE

Etiquette experts have come up with some categories for dressing that can help you figure out what is appropriate to wear in different situations. Business dress is generally a suit and tie for men and a suit with jacket and skirt or a tailored dress for women. Business casual is slightly less dressy, such as nice slacks and button-up shirt or sweater, but no jacket and tie, for men, and pants and sweater or nice blouse or a less tailored dress for women. Casual dress allows for nice (not worn or torn) jeans and can include well-pressed t-shirts (without slogans or pictures).

mouth—and you may not even realize that you are saying it.

The basics of appropriate dress in most Western cultures are pretty easy for us to understand. You may not go to an office every day, but you may know something about the rules for office attire. They are pretty easy to adapt to most situations, even those involving people from different cultures.

Most religious services call for something much like business dress, though some churches and synagogues these days encourage a "come as you are" vibe. If in doubt, you can't go wrong by wearing a nice dress or jacket and tie to church. People no longer wear only black to funerals, but it is a good idea to respect the mourners by avoiding bright colors and very flashy jewelry when attending funerals. Graduations and award ceremonies call for business dress. Occasions that

What you choose to wear can say a lot about your personality, and help signal what you are like. Just be sure you're sending the signals you want.

involve formal invitations, such as weddings or proms, often involve formal dress—a suit and tie for men and dressy dress for women. If the invitation says black tie, men should wear a tuxedo and women an evening gown or dressy cocktail dress. If you are planning to attend an event and do not know what you are expected to wear, it is fine to ask the person who invited you or the sponsors of the event.

If you are invited to an event of a culture that you are unfamiliar with, ask the person who invited you what you are expected to wear. For the most part, though, as long as you are in the United States, Western business dress will send the message that you respect your hosts and the event you are attending, even if the other people there are attired in something more appropriate to their culture. It is far better to wear what is considered respectful in your own culture than to try to mimic someone else's style of dress and not get it right. Traditional clothing can convey messages you don't understand, and you might inadvertently give offense when your intention was just the opposite. When in doubt, ask your host.

THE BAREFOOT GUEST

If you've figured out what clothes to wear, what shoes to wear should be pretty simple. But in some cases, the question is not what shoes to wear, but whether to wear shoes at all. Many

These young Jews are praying at the Western Wall in Jerusalem. Some Jewish men wear yarmulkes when they are in public or when they pray.

Asians (and some Russians and some people in Hawaii) remove their shoes when entering homes. If you visit someone's home and see that shoes have been placed outside the door, that's your signal to take off your shoes before going inside. This will be a nice gesture of respect to your hosts. Don't worry if your socks have holes or don't match—they'll appreciate the gesture anyway.

In some cultures, people wear specific, and, to other cultures, unusual clothing. For example, many Muslim women cover all but their faces; some Hindus may wear scarves that have religious significance. Orthodox Jewish men wear yarmulkes, small caps that fit on the crown of the skull. When you encounter people wearing traditional clothing that seems strange to you, it is important to be respectful. People's cultural dress is important to them, and it likely has deep significance. It is poor manners indeed to make someone feel uncomfortable because of what he or she is wearing.

MYTHS AND FACTS

MYTH: There are only a couple of cultures that are different from the main one in my community.

FACT: Culture is not defined just by race or ethnicity. You probably encounter many different cultures every day, and people usually belong to more than one culture.

MYTH: All Muslims are Arabs.

FACT: More than a billion people practice the Islamic faith, and only 15 to 20 percent of these people are from the Middle East.

MYTH: People from different cultures will never understand one another.

FACT: People of many different cultures live mostly in harmony in many parts of the world. When people make an effort to understand and welcome the many different cultures that live together, they do find ways to overcome differences. Cultural understanding takes effort, but it is by no means a lost cause.

CHAPTER FIVE

CELEBRATE!

The differences among cultures show up most profoundly at times of celebration. More than anything else, except perhaps for language, holidays are embedded in the cultures that celebrate them. If you want to truly understand a culture, the best place to look is at their celebrations.

THANKSGIVING

In the United States, Thanksgiving is so widely celebrated that people who have lived there all their lives tend to forget that Pilgrims, turkeys, and pumpkin pie do not adorn tables worldwide at the end of November. However, most cultures do have some sort of celebration of thanksgiving, often in the autumn (to coincide with the harvest) or in the spring (to celebrate having survived the winter).

Thanksgiving is a fun holiday, but people who are far from home can feel homesick and isolated when the people around them are gathering with family and friends and feasting on their traditional foods. Many families invite people who don't have relatives nearby to share their celebration. If you have guests from other cultures, it is a nice idea to acknowledge their cultures when you invite them to your feast. Remember that the Thanksgiving celebrated by the Pilgrims in colonial America was a multicultural meal. The colonists invited the natives to share their harvest celebration to express their gratitude to the natives for helping the colonists survive the winter. It is only fitting that the descendants of those colonists offer to share their celebration with today's newcomers. That is a great way to show thankfulness.

If you have Thanksgiving guests from other cultures, ask them what foods they would like to eat. You can offer to pre-pare a favorite dish from their cultures, or they might like to bring a traditional dish to share with you and your family. You

An ideal holiday feast makes everyone at the table feel welcomed and valued. There's something for everybody at this holiday feast.

don't have to pass on the turkey and stuffing (or the pie!), but don't limit your celebration to your own traditions. Ask your guests too about any other traditions they might enjoy—such as games or decorations—that will make them feel welcome.

RAMADAN

Ramadan is a special and deeply spiritual holiday for Muslims. It commemorates the revealing of the Quran to the prophet Muhammad. It is a month-long time of prayer and fasting, observed during the ninth month of the Islamic calendar, which falls about ten days earlier each year according to the Gregorian calendar. Muslims pray, read the Quran, and fast from dawn to sunset during the entire month of Ramadan. If you have friends who are observant Muslims, don't expect them to join you for an after-school slice of pizza during Ramadan.

The Quran is a beautiful piece of literature and the primary religious text of Islam. Muslims believe that God revealed the Quran to the prophet Muhammad via the angel Gabriel.

KWANZAA

Many African Americans celebrate Kwanzaa for the seven days from December 26 through January 1. Kwanzaa was established in 1966 to honor African American culture and heritage. Kwanzaa celebrates life, family, and community. Each of the seven days is devoted to a particular value: unity, self-determination, collective work and responsibility, cooperative economics, purpose, creativity, and faith. During Kwanzaa, people greet each other by asking, "Habari gani?" a Swahili phrase that means "What's the news?" A different answer is given for each day. If you have friends who celebrate Kwanzaa, you can say "Habari gani," and then ask for an explanation of the answer. Your friends will be happy that you asked and delighted to explain.

HAPPY HOLIDAYS

What do you say? Happy holidays? Merry Christmas? Habari gani? Happy Hanukkah? Or do you give up and just say "bah humbug"? Using the right greeting during the holiday season is not as hard as some people make it sound. If you know the tradition of the person you're greeting and you know that it is holiday time for them (and keep in mind that some holidays move around the calendar), then offer the appropriate greeting. If you don't know what's appropriate, it's fine to just say "happy holidays." Making an effort to acknowledge and respect the traditions of others isn't a political statement. It's kindness and courtesy.

EASTER

Easter is the major holiday in the Christian tradition. Hispanics are especially likely to have a big celebration at Easter. While Easter is associated with many secular activities and traditions celebrating the return of spring, such as egg hunts and chocolate bunnies, for Christians it is a deeply spiritual celebration of the resurrection of Christ. Easter falls in the spring, always on a Sunday. Christians attend church services on Easter morning, and then usually gather for a feast afterwards. Christians vary in how they celebrate Easter, so if you are invited to an Easter service (and it is common for Christians to invite friends), ask your host to explain beforehand what you are and are not expected to do.

PASSOVER

This holiday, which falls in the spring, is an eight-day festival celebrating the escape of the Israelites from slavery in ancient Egypt. On the first two nights of Passover, Jews celebrate with a special feast, called a Seder. Even if you are not Jewish, you may still be invited to a Seder because it is traditional to invite non-Jews and to treat strangers like members of the family. Seder feasts involve foods with special meanings, and a lot of rituals are observed. But don't be intimidated if you don't know what's going on. Guests are allowed, even encouraged, to ask questions. Just follow the lead of your host and be polite, and you'll learn a lot and make new friends.

CHAPTER SIX

LET'S EAT

Most cultures define themselves, at least in part, by when and how they gather around the table, and what and how they eat when they get there. As we saw in the last chapter, most holidays involve either eating or avoiding it. So if you want to develop a keen sense of cross-cultural etiquette, grab a fork, chopsticks, or a piece of naan and discover what and how different cultures eat.

TABLE MANNERS

You may have been told throughout your childhood to clean your plate, but membership in the clean plate club varies a great deal from culture to culture. Some people leave a little food on their plates as a gesture of politeness and acknowledgement that there is plenty. Others, such as Cambodians, use a clean plate as a signal that they want more food. So if you force in that last bite just to be polite, you might end up with an unwanted second serving! In Japan, cleaning your plate is a compliment to the host and suggests that the guest enjoyed the food.

In Europe, people do not generally rest their hands in their laps at the table as many people in the United States have been taught to do; instead they rest their wrists on the table when they are not actually eating. This practice may go back to premodern times when keeping your hands on the table made it clear that you weren't hiding a weapon.

In Asia, making noise while you eat—slurping your noodles, smacking, and burping at the table—is perfectly acceptable and shows that you are enjoying your food. In India, licking your fingers gives the same message. In Middle Eastern cultures, it is common to eat with your hands, sometimes using bread to scoop up other foods. In Muslim countries, people use only the right hand to eat (and reserve the left hand

If you didn't grow up using them, eating with chopsticks can be tricky. But it can also be a lot of fun.

for hygiene). In Asia, chopsticks are used in place of forks, and soup is often drunk out of the bowl.

Your best bet when eating with others is to watch what your fellow diners are doing and follow suit.

WHEN NOT TO SAY NO AND WHEN TO TAKE NO FOR AN ANSWER

One of the easiest ways to offend people is by refusing their offers of food. If the people offering to share their food are poor, you might reasonably think that the kindest thing to do would be to refuse. However, that is not usually the case. The

WHAT'LL YOU HAVE?

Individuals vary in how closely they adhere to their culture's practices around food, and there are many different sects within larger groups, but here are a few generalizations about food taboos. Hindus do not eat beef. Jews and Muslims do not eat pork. Many Jews do not mix meat and dairy or eat shellfish. Seventh-Day Adventists do not eat meat. Many Navajos avoid fish. Catholics avoid meat on certain holidays, such as Ash Wednesday and Fridays during Lent. Vegetarians eat animal products, such as milk, cheese, and eggs, but not the animals themselves. Vegans eat no animal products at all (including honey). Some people eat seafood but no other kind of meat.

best thing to do is to accept the generous offer, and then look for an opportunity to return the kindness. When people offer you food, they are making a gesture of kindness and opening their home and culture to you. To refuse to share their food is to reject not just the food, but the person who offers it and possibly their entire culture; the refusal could be taken as a serious insult.

So what happens when cultures clash? Say you are a vegetarian and a new friend from Cuba offers you *ropa vieja* (a traditional dish of shredded beef), or you are Jewish and a Spanish friend wants to share some chorizo, a spicy pork sausage commonly eaten in Spain. On one hand, you might feel that the gesture of kindness is more important than sticking to

Sharing food is one of the most common and often the most fun ways that people from different cultures get to know one another.

your normal observances. On the other hand, your commitment to your faith or your ethical practices might be too strong to make an exception. If that is the case, the best thing to do is explain as kindly as you can why you don't feel able to eat the food that has been offered (being extra careful not to express any judgment about the other person's food choices), and then suggest an alternative, such as "My religion forbids pork, but I would love to share some of your rice, if that is okay." You might also ask the person if he or she has any food taboos. What might have been a difference between you could turn into something you have in common. You might not share the same food traditions and taboos, but you both have some, and discussing them can be the start of a deeper understanding.

By the same token, never pressure someone to eat a food that is taboo in his or her culture. It may not seem to you like a big deal to break a food taboo, but for your friends (and their families) it might be a very big deal indeed.

The world is full of a great variety of people, and they have lots of traditions, practices, and habits. Learning about these different cultures and showing that you respect them isn't hard. In fact, it is the easiest thing you can do to help make the world a better, more peaceful, place.

GLOSSARY

Cajun A person descended from French Canadians who lives in the bayous of Louisiana, and the language and culture of these people.

cocktail dress A fancy dress that is short, yet suitable for formal occasions.

Creole A person whose ancestors were a mix of Europeans and blacks (especially Caribbean blacks), and the culture of these people.

culture The customs, beliefs, practices, and values of a given social group.

gender The cultural and behavior attributes associated with a particular sex.

gender gap The difference between the rights, opportunities, and expectations between and among the genders.

Gregorian calendar The calendar system devised in 1582 to bring the calendar back in line with the solar year, which is used by most of the world today.

Hispanic A person who comes from an area where Spanish is primarily spoken, particularly Latin America, or the culture of Spanish-speaking communities.

hygiene The practices of cleanliness in order to maintain good health.

Latino A person who lives in Mexico, Central America, or South America, or a person who lives in the United States but whose family is from Latin America.

Lent The period between Ash Wednesday and Easter when Christians fast and pray in preparation for Easter. It lasts about forty days.

LGBTQ An abbreviation for lesbian, gay, bisexual, transgender, and queer/questioning which is often used as an adjective referring to the people and cultures of people who are members of these categories. Also commonly given as LGBT.

microcosm Something that represents in a small way something much larger, the features or characteristics of something much larger.

Muhammad The founder of the religion of Islam.

naan A flat bread traditionally eaten in India.

orthodox Attitudes or beliefs that are in line with what has traditionally been considered true and acceptable in any given religion or culture.

Quran The sacred book of Islam; also Koran.

taboo Something that is not allowed.

tuxedo A dinner jacket worn on formal occasions.

vegan A person who neither eats nor uses animal products of any kind.

FOR MORE INFORMATION

Center for Intercultural Learning/Global Affairs Canada
Global Affairs Canada
125 Sussex Drive
Ottawa, ON K1A 0G2
Canada
Website: http://www.international.gc.ca/cil-cai/index.aspx?lang=eng
The Center for Intercultural Learning/Global Affairs Canada pro-
    vides cultural information on countries around the world.

Centro
1915 Chicago Avenue
Minneapolis, MN 55404
(612) 874-1412
Email: Infocenter@centromn.org
Website: http://www.centromn.org
Centro is an organization dedicated to the well-being and full partic-
    ipation of Latinos, through education and family engagement.

Intercultural Communication Institute
8835 SW Canyon Lane, Suite 238
Portland, OR 97225
(503) 297-4622
Email: Ici@intercultural.org
Website: http://intercultural.org
The ICI is a nonprofit organization with the mission of fostering an
    awareness and appreciation of cultural difference in both the
    international and domestic arenas.

Intercultural Dialog Institute
81 University Ave., Suite 711
Toronto, Ontario M5G 2E9
Canada
(416) 260-5885
Email: Info@interculturaldialog.com

Website: http://www.interculturaldialog.com
The Intercultural Dialog Institute is a nonprofit organization whose
purpose is to advance social cohesion through personal inter-
action by promoting respect and mutual understanding among
people of all cultures and faiths.

Teaching Tolerance
400 Washington Ave.
Montgomery, AL 36104
(888) 414-7752
Website: https://www.splcenter.org/teaching-tolerance
A project of the Southern Poverty Law Center, Teaching Tolerance
is a group dedicated to combatting prejudice among youth and
promoting equality, inclusiveness, and equitable learning envi-
ronments in the classroom.

UNESCO
7 Place Fontenoy
75007 Paris, France
=33 (0)1 4568 1000
Website: http://en.unesco.org/about-us/introducing-unesco
UNESCO is an organization that was established after World War II
to build networks among nations in order to promote solidarity
and peace.

WEBSITES

Because of the changing nature of internet links, Rosen Publishing has developed an online list of websites related to the
subject of this book. This site is updated regularly. Please use
this link to access the list:

http://www.rosenlinks.com/ER/cross

FOR FURTHER READING

Adiele, Faith. *Coming of Age Around the World: A Multicultural Antholo-gy.* New York, NY: New Press, 2007.

Blohm, Judith M. *Kids Like Me: Voices of the Immigrant Experience.* Boston, MA: Intercultural Press, 2006.

Budhos, Marina. *Remix: Conversations with Immigrant Teenagers.* Eu-gene, OR: Wipf & Stock, 2007.

Butler, Ester R. A., and Carol Leutenberg. *Teens—Accept and Em-brace Diversity.* Duluth, MN: Whole Persons Associates, 2014.

Dresser, Norine. *Multicultural Manners: Essential Rules of Etiquette for the 21st Century.* Hoboken, NJ: Wiley, 2006.

English, Suzanne-Marie. *The Etiquette of Kindness—It's Not Just About the Right Fork! Skills and Courtesies for Our Time.* Rescue, CA: Pleasant Ranch Publishing, 2012.

Gay, Kathlyn. *Cultural Diversity: Conflicts and Challenges the Ultimate Teen Guide.* Lanham, MD: Scarecrow Press, 2003.

Glossop, Jennifer. *The Kids Book of World Religions.* Toronto, ON: Kids Can Press, 2013.

Kalman, Bobbie. *Multicultural Meals.* Toronto, ON: Crabtree, 2003.

Kuiper, Kathleen. *The Culture of India.* New York, NY: Rosen Educa-tional Services, 2010.

Kuiper, Kathleen. *Islamic Art, Literature, and Culture.* New York, NY: Rosen Educational Services, 2010.

Lonely Planet Kids. *The Lonely Planet Kids Travel Book: Mind-Blowing Stuff on Every Country in the World.* Footscray, Victoria, Australia: Lonely Planet, 2015.

Madhi, Ali Akbar. *Teen Life in the Middle East.* Westport, CT: Green-wood Press, 2015.

Mooney, Carla. *Comparative Religion: Investigate the World Through Religious Tradition.* White River Junction, VT: Nomad Press, 2015.

Packer, Alex J. *How Rude! The Teen Guide to Good Manners, Proper Behavior, and Not Grossing People Out.* Minneapolis, MN: Free Spirit Publishing, 2014.

Smith, Daniel. *World Cultures Explained.* New York, NY: Rosen, 2015.

Webber, Diane. *Totally Tolerant: Spotting and Stopping Prejudice.* New York, NY: Franklin Watts, 2008.

BIBLIOGRAPHY

BBC. "Ramadan." July 5, 2011. (http://www.bbc.co.uk/religion/
    religions/islam/practices/ramadan_1.shtml).

China Highlights. "Do's and Don'ts in China." December 23, 2015
(http://www.chinahighlights.com/travelguide/guidebook/etiquette
    .htm).

Dresser, Norine. *Multicultural Manners: Essential Rules of Eti-
    quette for the 21st Century.* Hoboken, NJ: Wiley, 2006.

Fox, Sue. *Etiquette for Dummies.* Hoboken, NJ. Wiley, 2008.

Gardiner, Harry W., and Corinne Kosmitzki. *Lives Across Cultures.*
    London, UK: Pearson,
2010.

Gay, Kathlyn. *Cultural Diversity: Conflicts and Challenges the Ulti-
    mate Teen Guide.* Lanham, MD: Scarecrow Press, 2003.

Gelb, Connie. "Cultural Issues in the Higher Education Classroom."
    Student Pulse. Vol. 4 No. 7. 2012
(http://www.studentpulse.com/articles/661/2/cultural-
    issues-in-the-higher-education-classroom).

Global Exchange. "Myths About Islam." 2011
(http://www.globalexchange.org/resources/mideast/islam/myths).

Grise, Chrisanne. "Dining Manners Around the World." *Parents.*
    2013
(http://www.parents.com/kids/responsibility/manners/dining-
    manners-around-the-world).

International Business Center. "Latin America Etiquette and Cul-
    ture." 2012 (http://www.cyborlink.com/besite/latin_america
    .htm).

International Business Center. "Middle East Business Etiquette and
    Culture." 2012 (http://www.cyborlink.com/besite/mideast.htm).

Inter-Parliamentary Union. "Women in National Parliaments." April
    1, 2016 (http://www.ipu.org/wmn-e/classif.htm).

Kwintessential. "Etiquette and Protocol Guides." 2016
(http://www.kwintessential.co.uk/etiquette/doing-business-in.html).

National Council on Disability. "Common Myths About Diversity
    and Cultural Competency." 2006 (https://www.ncd.gov/

publications/2006/june2006).

Official Kwanzaa Website. "Kwanzaa: A Celebration of Family, Community, and Culture." 2016 (http://www. officialkwanzaawebsite.org/index.shtml).

PBS "Global Connections: The Middle East." 2002 (http://www.pbs.org/wgbh/globalconnections/mideast/questions/ women).

Pew Research Center. "Preference for the terms 'Hispanic' and 'Latino." October 21, 2013 (http://www.pewhispanic. org/2013/10/22/three-fourths-of hispanics-say-their-community-needs-a-leader/ph-hispanic-leader-10-2013-03-04).

Post, Peggy. *Emily Post's Etiquette.* New York, NY: William Morrow, 2011.

Ross, Meghan. "Plan Your Thanksgiving Around Different Cultures." Care. 2016 (https://www.care.com/a/plan-your-thanksgiv-ing-around-different-cultures-1309181319).

St. John, Warren. "The Politics of Good Touch, Bad Touch." *The New York Times.* July 23, 2006 (http://www.nytimes. com/2006/07/23/fashion/sundaystyles/23touch.html?_r=1&).

Thomas, David C. *Cultural Intelligence: Living and Working Globally.* San Francisco, CA: Berrett-Koehler Publishers, 2009.

Union for Reform Judaism. "Hanukkah." 2016 (http://www.reform-judaism.org/jewish-holidays/hanukkah).

University of Pennsylvania, African Studies Center. "Kwanzaa, What Is It?" March 1990. (https://www.africa.upenn.edu/K-12/ Kwanzaa_What_16661.html).

University of the Pacific Multicultural Studies. "What's Up with Culture?" (http://www2.pacific.edu/sis/culture).

Wyse Travel Confederation. "ITB World Travel Trends Report 2013/2014." December 2013 (https://wysetc.files.wordpress. com/2013/12/wttr_report_2014_web.pdf).

INDEX

46

ABOUT THE AUTHOR

Avery Elizabeth Hurt writes books and articles for children and young adults. She moved often when she was a child, and many people in many cultures made her feel welcome. She now tries to do that for others.

PHOTO CREDITS

Cover (top), p. 35 sutichak/iStock/Thinkstock; cover (bottom) Tom Merton/Caiaimage/Getty Images; p.5 SerrNovik/iStock/Thinkstock; pp. 7, 13, 18, 23, 29, 34 (top) Rawpixel.com/Shutterstock.com; p. 7 (bottom) Monkey Business Images/Shutterstock.com; pp. 10-11 © iStockphoto.com/Maestro-Books; p. 14 © iStockphoto.com/Christopher Futcher; p. 16 Jetta Productions/DigitalVision/Thinkstock; p. 19 Stephen Lovekin/WireImage/Getty Images; p. 20 diego cervo/iStock/Thinkstock; p. 21 hammett79/iStock/Thinkstock; p. 23 (bottom) Jupiterimages/Stockbyte/Thinkstock; p. 25 Hill Street Studios/Blend Images/Thinkstock; p. 26 © iStockphoto.com/Magdalena Jankowska; p. 30 © iStockphoto.com/mediapho-tos; p. 31 © iStockphoto.com/Arsela; p. 37 nixki/iStock/Think-stock.

Designer: Michael Moy; Editor: Heather Moore Niver; Photo Researcher: Heather Moore Niver